Iain Spragg
& Adrian Clarke

LEWIS HAMILTON

Bath · New York · Singapore · Hong Kong · Cologne · Delhi · Melbourne

Contents

GO GO The

boy racer

Formula One has found itself a new phenomenon in the shape of 22-year-old McLaren Mercedes driver Lewis Hamilton. Little known outside Grand Prix until early 2007, the rookie driver has quite simply stunned the sporting world with a succession of brilliant performances, tearing up the record books in the process. But the road to fame has been far from short, beginning way back in 1993 when an eager eight-year-old began competing in go-kart races at his local Hertfordshire track. It quickly became apparent that the youngster was a natural.

Making of a legend

Born in Stevenage, Hertfordshire, on January 7, 1985, Lewis Hamilton had an instant attraction to cars from a very young age. So much so in fact that his father Anthony and stepmother Linda spent three quarters of their monthly salary on a £1,000 go-kart for his Christmas present at the age of just six. Within two years the car-mad youngster was ready to take to the track and young Lewis soon began competing in local karting events. Within two years Hamilton had swept all before him in his age bracket, winning the prestigious McLaren Champions of the Future series. Racing was an expensive business, however, and with a modest income his parents struggled to support their son's interest. But with extreme faith in Lewis, proud dad Anthony worked three different jobs to make sure his boy had the best possible opportunity to develop his natural talent.

By the age of 10, Hamilton was already a highly-rated karting driver-winning several major competitions at junior level. The naturally gifted youngster (below) was driven to succeed and was already dreaming of a career in Formula One when he left school.

Hamilton's progress as an emerging talent hadn't gone unnoticed by the Formula One hierarchy and it wasn't long before the 10-year-old was introduced to McLaren boss Ron Dennis. The youngster is reported to have cheekily said on that first meeting: "I'm going to race for you one day. I'm going to race for McLaren." The team supremo kept a close eye on his progress, seeing him win the Super One British Championship (1995 and 1997), the Sky TV Kart Masters Championship (1996) and the Champions of the Future series (1996 and 1997). Hamilton's reputation within the racing fraternity was growing fast and it was clear that the teenager possessed a special talent behind the wheel that set him apart from his peers. Lewis Hamilton was being earmarked for bigger and better things. His lifelong dream of becoming a professional racing driver was looking like it might really become a reality.

Just days before the 2007 British Grand Prix at Silverstone, Lewis Hamilton returned to the Daytona go-karting circuit in Milton Keynes, the scene of some of his greatest triumphs as a junior karting champion. On hand to give coaching tips to a select group of children competing at the British Racing Drivers 'Stars of Tomorrow' event, it was obvious that Hamilton has nothing but fond memories of his karting days. "This is where I learnt my racing craft," he told the awe-struck youngsters. "The manoeuvres you see me use in F1, I wouldn't have had without karting."

It seems that Hamilton's rapid rise to stardom in 2007 has already had a major impact on the number of kids looking to take part in motor sport at a young age. The Daytona track has doubled the number of children racing there within the last 12 months to 5,000 and much of that has been put down to the 'Lewis Hamilton effect'. As well as passing on advice to the future stars of Formula One (above right), the Grand Prix star also presented the winner's trophy to 11-year-old Suffolk driver Alex Albon (left), winner of the day's event.

A star in waiting *1998*

JOINING A WINNING TEAM

Sensing that they might have a future world champion on their hands as early as 1998, Team McLaren signed Lewis Hamilton up to their driver development support programme. The financial burden previously carried by his family was now taken up by the team, who included an option in his contract stating that he had a future drive in their F1 car. This made 13-year-old Hamilton the youngest ever driver to secure a Formula One contract. The teenager's progress grew apace – despite the security guaranteed him by the contract – as the Hertfordshire-born prodigy continued to lift a series of major international titles. The 1999 season saw Hamilton become Intercontinental A champion and Junior ICA Vice European champion. A maximum points total gave him the Formula A European Championship the following year, while shortly after he was named as karting's world number one.

McLaren Mercedes announce that 21-year-old GP2 champion Lewis Hamilton will join their Formula One team for the 2007 season (left). The highly-rated driver immediately impressed the team management with some excellent displays in testing for the new season. (right)

At 16, McLaren decided to hand their most prized asset a seat in a racing car for the first time and it didn't take long for the youngster to adapt to life after karting, finishing a creditable fifth in the British Formula Renault series. Within two years he'd captured the title and in 2004 he was promoted to the F3 Euroseries. After two seasons he was champion again, at the tender age of 20.

(Top left) Hamilton celebrates his seat in the 2007 McLaren Mercedes car with team boss Ron Dennis. (Above and right) Mika Hakkinen and David Coulthard were the two McLaren drivers when Hamilton joined the team in 1998.

Hamilton gives fans the thumbs-up after lifting the GP2 series at the first attempt in 2006 for the ART team. Next stop Formula One!

GP2 Series
2005

After dominating Formula Three in 2005, Hamilton won a seat on the highly-rated ART Grand Prix GP2 team. It was to prove a sensational season for the rising star as he won the championship with ease at the first attempt. With five wins to his name, including a double at Silverstone before the 2006 British Grand Prix, and a triumph on the streets of Monte Carlo, it was apparent that McLaren's leading prospect's development had come as far as it could go before they unleashed him on Formula One. At 21, it was seen as a gamble to hand one of their prized seats to an inexperienced rookie, but boss Ron Dennis had seen enough to know that it was a gamble he was prepared to take.

(Top) The 21-year-old rushes straight towards father Anthony after clinching the GP2 title at Monza. (Middle) Hamilton poses with the trophy after his second place at Monza clinched him the GP2 World Championship. (Bottom) The GP2 champion is a dab hand with the champagne on the podium. (Main Left) Young Lewis Hamilton is already in the sights of Formula One star Felipe Massa.

(Top) With father Anthony and younger brother Nicholas at the Autosport Awards dinner. (Middle) Fernando Alonso gets to know his new team-mate as they compare mobile phones at the launch of the team's new car. (Right) Hamilton tears around the streets of Valencia at the launch of the new Vodafone McLaren Mercedes car in January 2007 (overleaf).

Awards and rewards *2007*

Ever since he had sat in his first go-kart 15 years earlier, Lewis Hamilton had dreamed of being a Formula One driver. At the tender age of 22, that dream was finally fulfilled. He'd achieved everything possible in motor sport below Grand Prix level and had proved beyond any doubt that he was capable of making the big step up. It was time for Hamilton to join the big boys.

A formula

one rookie

Hamilton appeared to be extremely relaxed ahead of his debut race, sharing an inflatable boat ride with team-mate Fernando Alonso on St Kilda beach and chatting to Australian cricket legend Shane Warne in the McLaren Mercedes garage ahead of his final qualifying session for the Melbourne Grand Prix.

ALBERT PARK

The talking was finally over and Hamilton's moment of truth had arrived. The young Englishman's dream of becoming a Formula One driver became reality on Melbourne's Albert Park street circuit, where all eyes were on McLaren's hotshot. After a shaky final qualifying session, the youngster claimed fourth place on the grid, two places behind world champion Fernando Alonso. But the race itself, watched over a 100,000 fans, was all that mattered to Lewis.

AUSTRALIAN GRAND PRIX
Albert Park

Circuit length: **5.303km**
Number of laps: **58**
Race length: **307.574km**
Lap Record: **1min 24.125sec**
(M Schumacher Ferrari 2004)

FIRST FOUR ON THE GRID
Pole: **Raikkonen** 2: **Alonso** 3: **Heidfeld** 4: **Hamilton**

FIRST EIGHT TO FINISH PLUS CHAMPIONSHIP POINTS
Winner: **Raikkonen** (Fin) Ferrari **10**
Second: **Alonso** (Spn) McLaren Mercedes **8**
Third: **Hamilton** (GB) McLaren-Mercedes **6**
Fourth: **Heidfeld** (Ger) BMW Sauber **5**
Fifth: **Fisichella** (Ita) Renault **4**
Sixth: **Massa** (Bra) Ferrari **3**
Seventh: **Rosberg** (Ger) Williams-Toyota **2**
Eighth: **R Schumacher** (Ger) Toyota **1**

It was the stuff of dreams for Hamilton as he passed team-mate Alonso on the first corner, bravely outmanoeuvring the Spaniard – a move that propelled him into third place. The debutant briefly led the race on two occasions but his car couldn't quite match the pace of Raikkonen's Ferrari and that of Alonso over the distance. But a faultless drive and a comfortable third place finish earned Hamilton huge praise from all quarters.

Hamilton became the first F1 driver to claim a podium finish on his debut since Jacques Villeneuve in 1996 and was thrilled with his performance. Afterwards he said: "I'm absolutely ecstatic – today's result is more than I ever dreamed of achieving on my Grand Prix debut. A big thank you to the team who have worked so hard to make sure I was as prepared as I possibly could be."

Malaysian Grand Prix
Sepang *8 April 2007*

In steaming hot conditions, Hamilton produced yet another magical start in Kuala Lumpur, flying past Felipe Massa and Kimi Raikkonen before the opening bend. Despite severe pressure from the two experienced drivers in his rear view mirror, the 22-year-old held his nerve to claim a well deserved second place behind defending champion Fernando Alonso. Hamilton's magnificent drive marked him out as someone truly special.

MALAYSIAN GRAND PRIX
Sepang

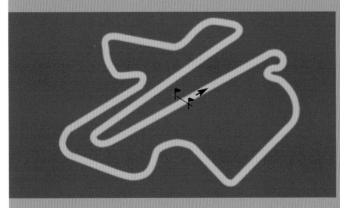

Circuit length:	5.543km
Number of laps:	56
Race length:	310.408km
Lap Record:	1min 34.223sec
	(Montoya Williams-BMW 2004)

FIRST FOUR ON THE GRID

Pole: **Massa** 2: **Alonso** 3: **Raikkonen** 4: **Hamilton**

FIRST EIGHT TO FINISH PLUS CHAMPIONSHIP POINTS

Winner:	**Alonso** (Spn) McLaren-Mercedes **10**
Second:	**Hamilton** (GB) McLaren-Mercedes **8**
Third:	**Raikkonen** (Fin) Ferrari **6**
Fourth:	**Heidfeld** (Ger) BMW Sauber **5**
Fifth:	**Massa** (Bra) Ferrari **4**
Sixth:	**Fisichella** (Ita) Renault **3**
Seventh:	**Trulli** (Ita) Toyota **2**
Eighth:	**Kovalainen** (Fin) Renault **1**

A perfectly executed strategy by the team and two excellent drives from Fernando Alonso and Lewis Hamilton secured an ecstatic McLaren Mercedes their 41st one-two finish. At the press conference Hamilton described the day's events as the "toughest race" of his career, while team boss Ron Dennis enthused about the youngster's impressive performance.

Hamilton's McLaren Mercedes whizzes past the spectacular grandstand tower at the Sepang circuit during qualifying for the Malaysian Grand Prix.

Bahrain Grand Prix

Sakhir

15 April 2007

Hamilton's sensational start to life as a Formula One driver had raised expectations ahead of the third race of the season in Bahrain, but in qualifying he seemed unfazed by the pressure – claiming second place on the starting grid behind Ferrari's Felipe Massa. Perhaps more significantly, the rookie out-qualified team-mate Alonso for the first time by more than 0.2 seconds. Suddenly the hype surrounding the Englishman began to reach fever pitch.

McLaren Mercedes mechanics work on Lewis Hamilton's car during the first of his two pit-stops during the 2007 Bahrain Grand Prix in Sakhir. Fortunately for the 22-year-old he didn't experience the same level of problems with car balance during the race as team-mate Alonso, who struggled throughout to grab fifth place.

Hamilton became the first driver in the history of Formula One to finish on the podium in all three of his first World Championship Grand Prix when finishing a strong second in Bahrain. Comfortably holding off the chasing pack despite encountering under-steer with his car, the talented driver pushed Ferrari's Felipe Massa all the way to the chequered flag, ending the race just 2.3 seconds behind the Brazilian winner. Hamilton's great display put him level at the top of the Drivers' Championship on 22 points alongside Alonso and Raikkonen.

BAHRAIN GRAND PRIX
Sakhir

Circuit length: **5.412km**

Number of laps: **57**

Race length: **308.238km**

Lap record: **1min 30.252sec**

(**M Schumacher Ferrari 2004**)

FIRST FOUR ON THE GRID

Pole: **Massa** 2: **Hamilton** 3: **Raikkonen** 4: **Alonso**

FIRST EIGHT TO FINISH PLUS CHAMPIONSHIP POINTS

Winner: **Massa** (Bra) Ferrari **10**

Second: **Hamilton** (GB) McLaren-Mercedes **8**

Third: **Raikkonen** (Fin) Ferrari **6**

Fourth: **Heidfeld** (Ger) BMW Sauber **5**

Fifth: **Alonso** (Spn) McLaren-Mercedes **4**

Sixth: **Kubica** (Pol) BMW Sauber **3**

Seventh: **Trulli** (Ita) Toyota **2**

Eighth: **Fisichella** (Ita) Renault 1

Spanish Grand Prix
Barcelona 13 May 2007

Good fortune was on Lewis' side at the start of the Spanish Grand Prix when team-mate Alonso was forced on to the gravel at the first corner – but after jumping from fourth to second on that first lap there was nothing lucky about the way he grasped his third consecutive second place finish. The result meant Hamilton led the Drivers' Championship after four races – and in doing so he became the youngest leader in the history of the competition, taking the record from team founder Bruce McLaren.

SPANISH GRAND PRIX
Barcelona

Circuit length: **4.655km**
Number of laps: **66**
Race length: **307.104km**
Lap record: **1min 22.680sec**
                  (Massa Ferrari 2007)

FIRST FOUR ON THE GRID
Pole: **Massa** 2: **Alonso** 3: **Raikkonen** 4: **Hamilton**

FIRST EIGHT TO FINISH PLUS CHAMPIONSHIP POINTS
Winner: **Massa** (Bra) Ferrari **10**
Second: **Hamilton** (GB) McLaren-Mercedes **8**
Third: **Alonso** (Spn) McLaren-Mercedes **6**
Fourth: **Kubica** (Pol) BMW Sauber **5**
Fifth: **Coulthard** (GB) Red Bull-Renault **4**
Sixth: **Rosberg** (Ger) Williams-Toyota **3**
Seventh: **Kovaleinen** (Fin) Renault **2**
Eighth: **Sato** (Jpn) Super Aguri-Honda **1**

Fernando Alonso looks unimpressed as Hamilton pours champagne down his neck on the podium at Catalunya, as race winner Massa attempts to soak the British star. The new championship leader said afterwards: "Things just keep on getting better and I continue living my dream. I'm happy with the outcome of the race and I want to keep on scoring points."

Monaco Grand Prix
Monte Carlo 27 May 2007

McLaren Mercedes duo Fernando Alonso and Lewis Hamilton made mincemeat of the demanding streets of Monte Carlo, dominating the 2007 Monaco Grand Prix from start to finish and lapping everyone except third-placed Brazilian Felipe Massa in his Ferrari. The young Brit tracked his team-mate closely throughout the race but with overtaking deemed too risky, he had to settle for yet a fourth consecutive second place in the Principality.

MONACO GRAND PRIX
Monte Carlo

Circuit length:	3.340km
Number of laps:	78
Race length:	260.520km
Lap record:	1min 14.439sec
	(M Schumacher Ferrari 2004)

FIRST FOUR ON THE GRID

Pole: **Alonso** 2: **Hamilton** 3: **Massa** 4: **Fisichella**

FIRST EIGHT TO FINISH PLUS CHAMPIONSHIP POINTS

Winner:	**Alonso (Spn) McLaren-Mercedes**	10
Second:	**Hamilton (GB) McLaren-Mercedes)**	8
Third:	**Massa (Bra) Ferrari**	6
Fourth:	**Fisichella (Ita) Renault**	5
Fifth:	**Kubica (Pol) BMW Sauber**	4
Sixth:	**Heidfeld (Ger) BMW Sauber**	3
Seventh:	**Wurz (Aus) Williams-Toyota**	2
Eighth:	**Raikkonen (Fin) Ferrari**	1

Hamilton's pace around the legendary street circuit was incredible, finishing over a minute ahead of Massa in third spot. Reportedly under team orders not to try and overtake Alonso, the young Englishman sat in behind the Spaniard from start to finish – a result that kept him on top of the drivers' championship.

Hamilton applauds winner Alonso on the Monte Carlo podium (top). The British star is presented with his second place trophy by Caroline, Princess of Hanover (middle). Actor Jude Law poses with the nation's newest sporting superstar in the pit lane (bottom).

Canadian Grand Prix
Montreal 10 June 2007

Just when Lewis Hamilton thought his debut season couldn't get any better, it did with a magnificently crafted victory at the Canadian Grand Prix in Montreal. After claiming the first pole position of his short career at the Gilles Villeneuve circuit, the rookie sensation led from start to finish and in doing so became the first black driver to win a Formula One Grand Prix. Robert Kubica's horrific crash and several other incidents during the race led to the safety car being employed on four occasions, but Hamilton refused to let it affect his concentration and produced a faultless drive. Team-mate Fernando Alonso had a nightmare race finishing seventh and bitterly described Hamilton's win as "very lucky" afterwards although most experts were full of praise for the Englishman.

Lewis gives the victory sign (top), having successfully completed the 70 laps starting and finishing in first position (above and opposite).

Hamilton's popularity began to reach fever pitch in Canada with Union Jack flags seen all around the Montreal circuit. The 22-year-old's humble and well-mannered personality off the track has unquestionably won him hordes of new fans both sides of the Atlantic, but there is no question that his brave racing style marks him out as a future world champion. Hamilton's parade car may have been number two but the rookie is already eyeing becoming Grand Prix's undisputed number one.

Pole position holder Hamilton waves to his legion of adoring fans in Montreal on the traditional pre-race drivers' parade around the Gilles Villeneuve circuit.

The young Englishman punches his fist with delight shortly after taking the chequered flag for the first time in his career – incredibly in only his sixth Formula One Grand Prix.

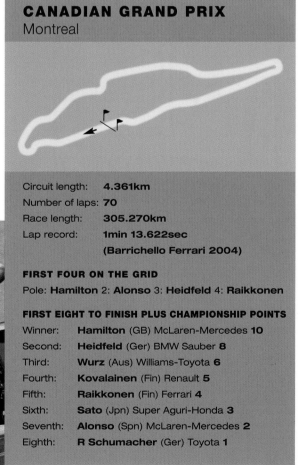

CANADIAN GRAND PRIX
Montreal

Circuit length: **4.361km**
Number of laps: **70**
Race length: **305.270km**
Lap record: **1min 13.622sec**
(Barrichello Ferrari 2004)

FIRST FOUR ON THE GRID
Pole: **Hamilton** 2: **Alonso** 3: **Heidfeld** 4: **Raikkonen**

FIRST EIGHT TO FINISH PLUS CHAMPIONSHIP POINTS

Winner:	**Hamilton** (GB) McLaren-Mercedes	**10**
Second:	**Heidfeld** (Ger) BMW Sauber	**8**
Third:	**Wurz** (Aus) Williams-Toyota	**6**
Fourth:	**Kovalainen** (Fin) Renault	**5**
Fifth:	**Raikkonen** (Fin) Ferrari	**4**
Sixth:	**Sato** (Jpn) Super Aguri-Honda	**3**
Seventh:	**Alonso** (Spn) McLaren-Mercedes	**2**
Eighth:	**R Schumacher** (Ger) Toyota	**1**

A thrilled Hamilton (left) leaps for joy as he returns to the McLaren-Mercedes garage after becoming the youngest driver to have won the Canadian Grand Prix. The exuberant celebrations showed just how much it meant to the young driver to complete his first win so early on in his Formula One career. Comparisons to the legendary Michael Schumacher, who won a record seven world titles, are already being made.

FORMULA 1° GRAND PRIX DU CANADA 2007

The Stevenage-born driver (top) jumps for joy. (Above) Lewis explains to the watching world how he achieved his maiden Grand Prix victory, flanked by surprise podium finishers Nick Heidfeld and Alexander Wurz.

It's smiles all round from the Englishman (right) on the winners' podium as he deservedly savours every second of his hard-fought victory in Montreal.

US Grand Prix
Indianapolis 17 June 2007

The incredible fairytale start to life in Formula One for Lewis Hamilton continued apace at the famous Indianapolis Motor Speedway circuit as the McLaren Mercedes star registered a second successive pole position and second race victory in a row. Pressed fiercely by team-mate Alonso throughout the 73-lap race, the British star kept his nerve superbly to open up a ten point lead at the top of the drivers' championship table.

US GRAND PRIX
Indianapolis

Circuit length: **4.192km**
Number of laps: **73**
Race length: **306.016km**
Lap record: **1min 10.399sec**
(Barrichello Ferrari 2004)

FIRST FOUR ON THE GRID
Pole: **Hamilton** 2: **Alonso** 3: **Massa** 4: **Raikkonen**

FIRST EIGHT TO FINISH PLUS CHAMPIONSHIP POINTS
Winner: **Hamilton** (GB) McLaren Mercedes **10**
Second: **Alonso** (Spn) McLaren-Mercedes **8**
Third: **Massa** (Bra) Ferrari **6**
Fourth: **Raikkonen** (Fin) Ferrari **5**
Fifth: **Kovalainen** (Fin) Renault **4**
Sixth: **Trulli** (Ita) Toyota **3**
Seventh: **Webber** (Aus) Red Bull-Renault **2**
Eighth: **Vettel** (Ger) BMW Sauber **1**

The Englishman gets to the first corner ahead of the field at the legendary Indianapolis circuit despite the best efforts of defending champion Fernando Alonso (left). Hamilton is calmness personified as he strolls along to the grid (centre).

Alonso's attempts to pass the championship leader on the outside are blocked by the determined young Brit (above).

UNITED STATES GRAND PRIX

For the second successive race Hamilton is first to take the chequered flag (main) in front of the packed grandstand. The Union Jack flag is raised as the youngster sings along to the national anthem on the podium at Indianapolis. (above)

French Grand Prix
Magny-Cours 1 July 2007

Stung by McLaren Mercedes' early season dominance, Ferrari were back on song at the French Grand Prix at Magny-Cours claiming a one-two finish, well ahead of third-placed Hamilton who kept up his amazing record of achieving a podium finish in every F1 race he's taken part in.

The championship leader was in a relaxed frame of mind as he joked with the world's assembled press in the paddock at Magny-Cours ahead of the eagerly-anticipated French Grand Prix.

Kimi Raikkonen's victory did little to alter the championship table however as Hamilton's closest challenger Alonso could only manage seventh after struggling with gearbox difficulties in qualifying.

FRENCH GRAND PRIX
Magny-Cours

Circuit length: **4.411km**
Number of laps: **70**
Race length: **308.586km**
Lap record: **1min 15.377sec**
                    (M Schumacher Ferrari 2004)

FIRST FOUR ON THE GRID
Pole: **Massa** 2: **Hamilton** 3: **Raikkonen** 4: **Kubica**

FIRST EIGHT TO FINISH PLUS CHAMPIONSHIP POINTS
Winner: **Raikkonen (Fin) Ferrari 10**
Second: **Massa (Bra) Ferrari 8**
Third: **Hamilton (GB) McLaren-Mercedes 6**
Fourth: **Kubica (Pol) BMW Sauber 5**
Fifth: **Heidfeld (Ger) BMW Sauber 4**
Sixth: **Fisichella (Ita) Renault 3**
Seventh: **Alonso (Spn) McLaren-Mercedes 2**
Eighth: **Button (GB) Honda 1**

Hamilton in action at Magny-Cours – but the English star found it difficult to keep pace with the likes of Raikkonen and Massa on French soil.

BRITISH GRAND PRIX
Silverstone

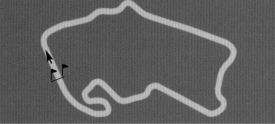

Circuit length: **5.141km**

Number of laps: **60**

Race length: **308.355km**

Lap record: **1min 18.739sec**

(M Schumacher Ferrari 2004)

FIRST FOUR ON THE GRID

Pole: **Hamilton** 2: **Raikkonen** 3: **Alonso** 4: **Massa**

FIRST EIGHT TO FINISH PLUS CHAMPIONSHIP POINTS

Winner: **Raikkonen** (Fin) Ferrari **10**

Second: **Alonso** (Spn) McLaren-Mercedes **8**

Third: **Hamilton** (GB) McLaren-Mercedes **6**

Fourth: **Kubica** (Pol) BMW Sauber **5**

Fifth: **Massa** (Bra) Ferrari **4**

Sixth: **Heidfeld** (Ger) BMW Sauber **3**

Seventh: **Kovalainen** (Fin) Renault **2**

Eighth: **Fisichella** (Ita) Renault **1**

British Grand Prix
Silverstone 8 July 2007

A dream qualifying lap helped Hamilton claim pole in front of his home fans, raising expectations that he would be the first British winner of the Silverstone Grand Prix since Damon Hill. It wasn't however to be as Ferrari's Kimi Raikkonen claimed the lead from the young Brit on lap 16 and never relinquished it. A frustrating afternoon for Hamilton also saw team-mate Fernando Alonso pip him for second place. Still, nine podium finishes out of nine isn't a bad way to start your Formula One career!

It was Hamilton-mania at Silverstone as over 200,000 fans flocked to the Northamptonshire circuit over the weekend to catch a glimpse of Britain's biggest new sporting hero.

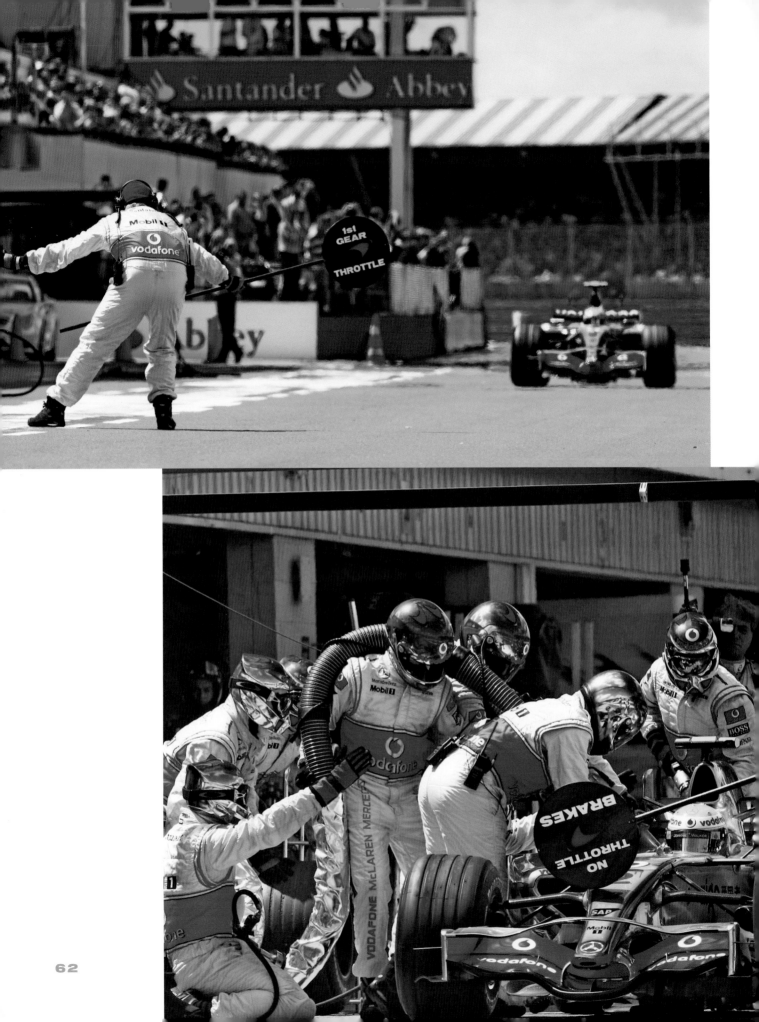

Despite his disappointment, Hamilton still enjoyed his ninth successive podium finish at Silverstone, soaking team-mate Alonso with yet another magnum of champagne. (above)

Hamilton's first pit stop (top left) cost him the lead to flying Finn Kimi Raikkonen on lap 16 and a rare mistake when reacting to the lollipop board in the pits also cost the rookie driver valuable time in his efforts to catch the leader. (bottom left)

Picture Credits

Getty Images: 10, 12t, 18b, 19, 20-21, 24br
Dave M. Benett/Getty Images: 18t, 43b
Philip Brown/Getty Images: 6-7
Robert Cianflone/Getty Images: 27
Michael Cooper/Getty Images: 12b, 13
Paul Gilham/Getty Images: 4-5, 8, 9, 15, 30, 31b, 32, 34-35, 36t, 38, 38m, 39, 41, 44t, 48tl, 49r, 60, 61r,
Bertrand Guay/Getty Images: 34l
Michael Heiman/Getty Images: 52
Pascal Le Segretain/Getty Images: 43t, 43m
Bryn Lennon/Getty Images: 33

Clive Mason/Getty Images: 2t, 17b, 17m, 42, 44b, 46
Clive Rose/Getty Images: 17t, 56, 57t, 58
Mark Thompson/Getty Images: 1, 2-3, 14b, 22-23, 24-25, 24bl, 26, 28-29, 36-37, 40t, 40b, 41t, 45, 48b, 49t, 50-51, 52r, 54b, 55r, 59, 62t, 62b, 63tr
Gabriel Bouys/AFP/Getty Images: 54t
Don Emmert/AFP/Getty Images: 53
Toshifumi Kitamura/AFP/Getty Images: 11
The Eng Koon/AFP/Getty Images: 31
Lars Baron/Bongarts/Getty Images:16

This is a Parragon Book

This edition first published in 2007

Parragon Books Ltd
Queen Street House
4 Queen Street
Bath BA1 1HE

ISBN 978-1-4075-2104-6

ENDEAVOUR LONDON LTD
info@endeavourlondon.com

This edition created by Endeavour London Ltd

Text: Iain Spragg and Adrian Clarke
Picture Research: Franziska Payer Crockett
Art Direction: Paul Welti
Design Realisation: Keith Holmes
Artworks: Keith Holmes
Project Coordinator: Liz Ihre

Printed in Poland